The
TOXICITY BIBLE
- FOR HIM -

ENGLISH STANDARD VERSION

Containing 100+ Ways To F*** With
Her Head!

ISBN: 9798376269763

The
TOXICITY BIBLE

If you can't change her.
Change her.

read that again

Stay Toxic 1:1

The
TOXICITY BIBLE

If a girl calls you daddy
and you're not feeling the
relationship, just tell her
you're going to get milk
and never come back.

Stay Toxic 1:2

The
TOXICITY BIBLE

If you're looking for
revenge, get a better
looking partner with the
same name.

Stay Toxic 1:3

The
TOXICITY BIBLE

She's texting you "He's
just a friend."

While some guy's in her
bed laughing at your text.

Stay Toxic 1:4

The
TOXICITY BIBLE

If she texts you "Good
morning, sorry I fell
asleep."

Reply "It's okay, I just
got home."

Stay Toxic 1:5

The
TOXICITY BIBLE

She thinks I'm hers,
but my friends call her
"which one".

Stay Toxic 1:6

The
TOXICITY BIBLE

If she cancels on you last
minute, do not cause a
scene.

Reply with "dw, I'll stick
to my first plan then,
have a good night."

Stay Toxic 1:7

She didn't leave you on seen, you left her speechless.

Stay Toxic 1:8

The
TOXICITY BIBLE

Cheat and if you feel
guilty you truly loved her,
if not then it just wasn't
meant to be.

Stay Toxic 1:9

The
TOXICITY BIBLE

"Sorry I ghosted you for
4 months, I was looking
for my charger."

Stay Toxic 1:10

The
TOXICITY BIBLE

Cheating once doesn't
make you a cheater.

I fixed my car once,
doesn't make me a
mechanic.

Stay Toxic 1:11

The
TOXICITY BIBLE

Her: "No P for you
  tonight."

Me: "No P FROM you
  tonight."

Stay Toxic 1:12

The
TOXICITY BIBLE

When you're favourite girl isn't replying, you entertain the ones you don't even want just for fun.

Stay Toxic 2:1

The
TOXICITY BIBLE

If she ever says "He's probably out cheating on me."

Just reply with "That was a lucky guess."

Stay Toxic 2:2

The TOXICITY BIBLE

If she tries to argue with
you, look disinterested
and reply only with "ok".

Watch her attitude
change. Women crave a
reaction!

Stay Toxic 2:3

The
TOXICITY BIBLE

"I lowered my standards
and you still couldn't
reach them."

Stay Toxic 2:4

The
TOXICITY BIBLE

"You better start acting
right, because the girl I
told you not to worry
about replies faster."

Stay Toxic 2:5

The
TOXICITY BIBLE

"You thought I was in love? Please, the only thing I loved was the attention."

Stay Toxic 2:6

The
TOXICITY BIBLE

"If I wanted this energy,
I would've messaged my
ex."

Stay Toxic 2:7

The
TOXICITY BIBLE

If she texts you saying "I miss you."

Reply with "If you acted right, you wouldn't have to."

Then hit up her best friend.

Stay Toxic 2:8

The
TOXICITY BIBLE

Always remind her by
saying "Remember who
wanted who first."

Stay Toxic 2:9

The
TOXICITY BIBLE

If she says "Sorry, I forgot
to text you last night."

Reply with "It's cool,
your competitors didn't."

Stay Toxic 2:10

The
TOXICITY BIBLE

Don't get on one knee for
a girl that doesn't
consistently get on two.

Stay Toxic 2:11

The
TOXICITY BIBLE

When she gives me
attitude, I want to leave
my phone unlocked on
the bed and show her
who the real savage is.

Stay Toxic 2:12

The
TOXICITY BIBLE

The next time a girl asks
for your number - give
her your ex's and tell her
your name is your ex's
new partners name.

Stay Toxic 3:1

The
TOXICITY BIBLE

Why are you begging her
to act right when you
have others asking
"When can I see you?"

Never chase, always
replace.

Stay Toxic 3:2

The
TOXICITY BIBLE

If an ex texts you "Hey, what's up?"

Respond with "My standards... BYE."

Stay Toxic 3:3

The
TOXICITY BIBLE

If the girl you're talking to says "I just want to be friends."

Respond with "Weren't we friends the whole time?"

Stay Toxic 3:4

The
TOXICITY BIBLE

"Keep treating me like an option and you'll see how many I have."

Stay Toxic 3:5

The
TOXICITY BIBLE

"Are we hanging out or not because your best friend is waiting for an answer from me."

Stay Toxic 3:6

The
TOXICITY BIBLE

"If you don't want to be
replaced, why are you
acting so replaceable?"

Stay Toxic 3:7

The
TOXICITY BIBLE

Warn her with "It only takes one picture to show you how many options I have."

Stay Toxic 3:8

The

TOXICITY BIBLE

"I set the bar on the floor
and you still couldn't
reach it."

Stay Toxic 3:9

The
TOXICITY BIBLE

"You just moved down
on the roster, I'm not
desperate enough for you
right now."

Stay Toxic 3:10

The
TOXICITY BIBLE

We should stop calling
women bitches.

Bitch means female dog,
and dogs are loyal.

Stay Toxic 3:11

The
TOXICITY BIBLE

If you haven't met your
soulmate yet, don't feel
bad.

Even the married ones
are still searching.

Stay Toxic 3:12

The
TOXICITY BIBLE

"I knew I picked the
wrong sister."

Stay Toxic 4:1

The
TOXICITY BIBLE

"I don't hate you because hate is a feeling and I feel absolutely nothing for you."

Stay Toxic 4:2

The

TOXICITY BIBLE

"Can't throw shade on my name if you used to moan to it."

Stay Toxic 4:3

The
TOXICITY BIBLE

If she says "k"

Reply "Damn, you put more effort in that text than our relationship."

Stay Toxic 4:4

The
TOXICITY BIBLE

"Treat me like a joke and
I'll leave you like it's
funny."

Stay Toxic 4:5

"You keep running back, so obviously I'm not the problem."

Stay Toxic 4:6

The
TOXICITY BIBLE

"My friends use your
name as an insult."

Stay Toxic 4:7

The
TOXICITY BIBLE

"You were supposed to
help me get over my ex,
not make me want her
more."

Stay Toxic 4:8

The
TOXICITY BIBLE

"You're being overly
emotional."

Stay Toxic 4:9

The
TOXICITY BIBLE

Next time you're holding
your girls hand,
remember she used that
hand to put her ex back
in when it slipped out.

Stay Toxic 4:10

The
TOXICITY BIBLE

Women have so much
evil in their blood it has
to be drained once a
month.

Stay Toxic 4:11

The
TOXICITY BIBLE

You happiness never
resides in one girl because
she's never yours.

It's just your turn.

Stay Toxic 4:12

The
TOXICITY BIBLE

If she turns her volume
down on her phone when
you're near her - she's for
the streets.

Stay Toxic 5:1

The
TOXICITY BIBLE

During an argument, tell
her you're not going to
be disrespected by
someone you lowered
your standards for.

Stay Toxic 5:2

The
TOXICITY BIBLE

When you tell a girl to
shut up and she says
"Make me!"

Does she want D or a
right hook?

Stay Toxic 5:3

The
TOXICITY BIBLE

With a single girl you're
competing with twenty
guys, whereas a taken girl
you're only competing
with one.

Work smarter.

Stay Toxic 5:4

If she ever told you what
she likes in bed,
remember another guy
showed her that.

Stay Toxic 5:5

The
TOXICITY BIBLE

Being single is nice, but I
do miss waking up seeing
her crying with my
phone in her hand.

Stay Toxic 5:6

The
TOXICITY BIBLE

The girls that say they
need a guy with a big
package and a lot of
money, really just need to
be tighter and get a job.

Stay Toxic 5:7

The
TOXICITY BIBLE

Hot girl summer is for
HOT GIRLS.

The rest need to wait for
Halloween.

Stay Toxic 5:8

The
TOXICITY BIBLE

Saw my ex when I was driving down the street.

Funny how "I'd hit that" changes meaning over the years.

Stay Toxic 5:9

The
TOXICITY BIBLE

She will break a good
guys heart and meet
someone like me and be
hurt.

That's called karma.

Stay Toxic 5:10

The
TOXICITY BIBLE

You lose money chasing bitches, but you don't lose bitches chasing money.

Stay Toxic 5:11

The
TOXICITY BIBLE

When you're the toxic
guy, most women will
stay obsessed with you.

But the nice guys get
cheated on.

Stay Toxic 5:12

The
TOXICITY BIBLE

If she messages "Sorry I
didn't reply, my phone
died last night."

Respond with "Any
feelings I had left for you
also died last night."

Stay Toxic 6:1

The
TOXICITY BIBLE

If you date a girl that has a lot of guy friends, it's gonna end badly.

Don't listen to the "I just get on better with guys" excuse.

Stay Toxic 6:2

The
TOXICITY BIBLE

Girls want honesty until
they ask you what you
like in bed and you reply
"Everything my ex did."

Stay Toxic 6:3

The
TOXICITY BIBLE

When you stop hooking up with a girl and they ask for an explanation to why you've stopped replying to their messages.

Just say "Your father left you without a reason, I just thought you'd be used to it."

Stay Toxic 6:4

The
TOXICITY BIBLE

"Don't get mad cause you caught me cheating. Obviously I was seeking something you were lacking, apologise and do better."

Stay Toxic 6:5

"I love our deep talks, I want to know exactly how he played you - so I can do worse."

Stay Toxic 6:6

The
TOXICITY BIBLE

Men don't have trust
issues.

We put it in a mouth full
of teeth, if that's not trust
I don't know what is.

Stay Toxic 6:7

The
TOXICITY BIBLE

If she cheated on you,
you deserve no sympathy,
cause you did something
far worse.

You trusted her.

Stay Toxic 6:8

My girlfriend told me to get in touch with my feminine side - so I cheated on her with my female bestie.

Stay Toxic 6:9

The
TOXICITY BIBLE

Send flowers to your
girlfriends work
anonymously.

If she doesn't tell you
about it, she's cheating.

Stay Toxic 6:10

The
TOXICITY BIBLE

You can laugh if a girl
ever calls you ugly.

Remember it takes them
hours painting their face
to get enough confidence
to even leave the house.

Stay Toxic 6:11

The
TOXICITY BIBLE

Having a high body
count is not a flex, but
making them all think
they are the one is.

Stay Toxic 6:12

The
TOXICITY BIBLE

When they tell you that
they're starting to see red
flags, remind them that
it's the colour of love.

Stay Toxic 7:1

The
TOXICITY BIBLE

If you date a girl for less than a month, she is not your ex - she was a 30 day free trial.

Stay Toxic 7:2

The
TOXICITY BIBLE

"You can't trust these
women, they promise you
forever then leave when
you cheat."

Stay Toxic 7:3

The
TOXICITY BIBLE

Don't get jealous if you see your ex with someone else.

We were always taught to give our used toys to the less fortunate.

Stay Toxic 7:4

The
TOXICITY BIBLE

Ignoring a girls past will
only ruin your future.

Stay Toxic 7:5

The
TOXICITY BIBLE

If she can say "LOL" without laughing, she can say "I love you" without meaning it.

Stay Toxic 7:6

The
TOXICITY BIBLE

Girls always post "Single" but never "Single and ran thru".

Babe, advertise the whole you.

Stay Toxic 7:7

The
TOXICITY BIBLE

If your girl can't cook
and you have a side piece
that can - it's not
cheating.

It's survival.

Stay Toxic 7:8

The
TOXICITY BIBLE

"My girl is so loyal, she doesn't even sleep with her husband."

Stay Toxic 7:9

The
TOXICITY BIBLE

I hate when a girl thinks
she played me.

It makes me wanna snitch
on myself.

Stay Toxic 7:10

The
TOXICITY BIBLE

If she uses "I'm tired" as
an excuse.

Be the gentleman, let her
sleep and go see someone
who's awake.

Stay Toxic 7:11

The
TOXICITY BIBLE

I knew we were going to make history when she told me she's never been cheated on.

Stay Toxic 7:12

The
TOXICITY BIBLE

She had a King - I
shuffled the deck and got
a joker.

Stay Toxic 8:1

The
TOXICITY BIBLE

Don't let your 9/10
girlfriend stop you from
finding your 10/10 wife.

Stay Toxic 8:2

The
TOXICITY BIBLE

She wants a boyfriend,
but has seen more boxers
drop than Mike Tyson.

Stay Toxic 8:3

The
TOXICITY BIBLE

Sometimes you have to
cheat twice to make sure
she is the one.

Stay Toxic 8:4

The
TOXICITY BIBLE

Text her best friend on her phone saying "IM PREGNANT!"

If they reply "By who?"

She's cheating.

Stay Toxic 8:5

She said she faked it in bed.

That's cool, I faked everything to get you there.

Stay Toxic 8:6

The
TOXICITY BIBLE

If you try and be her soulmate, she'll replace and forget you.

But if you're her most toxic ex, she will talk about you in therapy for the rest of her life.

Stay Toxic 8:7

The
TOXICITY BIBLE

Text her "I miss us" and
never reply again.

Stay Toxic 8:8

The
TOXICITY BIBLE

Spray a cologne in her car
that's not yours and start
an argument.

Now you have a free
reason to cheat.

Stay Toxic 8:9

The TOXICITY BIBLE

Think of girls like shoes,
it's kinda silly to have
just one.

Stay Toxic 8:10

The
TOXICITY BIBLE

My girlfriend told me
"behind every successful
man is a woman."

So she's basically saying
more women = more
success.

Stay Toxic 8:11

The
TOXICITY BIBLE

Remember, God made
the perfect girl for Adam
and she still did him
wrong.

Stay Toxic 8:12

The
TOXICITY BIBLE

Don't block your ex on socials, let her see you post with the girls you told her not to worry about.

Stay Toxic 9:1

The
TOXICITY BIBLE

Don't over text.

Instead of sending five
messages to one girl, send
one message to five girls.

Stay Toxic 9:2

The
TOXICITY BIBLE

She told me she liked
Halloween and scary
stuff.

So I ghosted her.

Stay Toxic 9:3

The
TOXICITY BIBLE

On April 1st, confess to
her all the girls you've
cheated on her with.

After she's cried tell her
"April fools."

Stay Toxic 9:4

The
TOXICITY BIBLE

Don't argue with her, just
say "You sound just like
my ex" and walk away.

Stay Toxic 9:5

The
TOXICITY BIBLE

Why do girls say "Go talk to your hoes."

Like they think they are different and aren't one of them.

Stay Toxic 9:6

The
TOXICITY BIBLE

You should treat sleeping with girls as just a sport.

It's seen as more humane, like catch and release fishing.

Stay Toxic 9:7

The
TOXICITY BIBLE

If she plays hard to get,
once you get it - play
hard to contact.

Stay Toxic 9:8

The
TOXICITY BIBLE

Don't be stupid.

If she wants "a break",
she has someone waiting.

Stay Toxic 9:9

The
TOXICITY BIBLE

Statistics show that 86% of relationships end in breakup.

Don't stay loyal and pass up good P for 14% chance of success.

It's basic math.

Stay Toxic 9:10

The
TOXICITY BIBLE

If you have to ask for
head, she shouldn't have
to ask why you cheated.

Stay Toxic 9:11

The
TOXICITY BIBLE

You can make a hoe a
housewife, but you can't
make a housewife a hoe.

Stay Toxic 9:12

DISCLAIMER

This book was created solely for satire purposes and do not condone any malicious use or intent.

Toxicity in a relationship can cause irreparable harm, eroding trust and respect. It creates a negative and unhappy environment, making it difficult to rebuild the relationship. When people engage in toxic behaviour, it normalises the perpetual such behaviour in others.

Toxicity in a relationship can have far-reaching consequences, affecting not just the individuals involved but also their friends and family. It can take a toll on one's mental and emotional well-being, causing stress, anxiety, depression, and low self-esteem.

It often creates a vicious cycle of negative behaviour that can be difficult to break and limits growth and self-improvement. But most of all it destroys love and affection that once existed between two people, making it difficult to rekindle.

Therefore it is better to strive for kindness, respect, and healthy communication in all forms of relationships.

Made in United States
Cleveland, OH
17 December 2024

12094226R00066